GW00673692

Big Active

Editor &
Design director
Gerard Saint

Artist interviews
Daniel Mason

Text editor
Mark Reynolds

Cover
Homage to 'Lovesexy'
Art direction and design:
Gerard Saint and Mat Maitland
Photography: Patrick Ibanez
Photomontage: Mat Maitland
Boy and girl modelled by Wade
Crescent and Margo Stilley
Production: Bianca Redgrave

Die Deutsche Bibliothek
lists this publication in the
Deutsche Nationalbibliografie;
detailed bibliographic data is
available at http://dnb.ddb.de.

Published by
Die Gestalten Verlag
Berlin · London
ISBN 3-89955-060-9

Printed by Medialis Offsetdruck
GmbH, Berlin.
Made in Germany

For your local dgv
distributor, see
www.die-gestalten.de

Head
Heart
Hips &

The Seductive World of Big Active

Hello

Big-Active Limited

Fuck off

Big-Active Limited

**Business Cards
Circa 1990**
First impressions count
for so much. Based upon
children's 'speak and
spell' cards, Big Active's
early introductions were
designed to be straight-
talking and to the point.
One of the cards was
primarily reserved for
unwanted sales reps.

Introduction

COMMERCIAL ART by its very nature seeks to be seductive. It teases us and plays games with our senses. It stimulates hidden triggers of desire. It confounds, intrigues and irritates. It expresses a need to connect and communicate. Sometimes it grabs you by the balls, forces your attention and dares you to fall in love. Other times it whispers and teases, arousing profound feelings of empathy, recognition and understanding.

Head, Heart and Hips is a snapshot of Big Active. As art directors and designers we have always looked to create graphics for commissioned projects that reflect our attitude towards the things that turn us on. Over the years we have been enticed by the work of a great number of new and influential image-makers, both illustrators and photographers, many of whom have collaborated on our creative journey. A select group of these artists have come to be represented by Big Active, and this creative synergy with the core design team forms an essential part of the studio's aesthetic. In the wider view, Big Active brings together a vibrant group of like-minded visual conspirators who enjoy the thrill of seducing the world with their images.

This book is a sideways look inside our world. Playing with the idea of seduction and of sensual pleasures, we present an intuitive take on the sexier aspects of our commercial art. As well as a behind-the-scenes view of the themes that drive and inspire us, this book also features specially commissioned new work and remixes by our associated artists. Sometimes provocative, always stimulating and revealing, each represents a characteristic visual signature. This colourful landscape of ideas and styles conspires to shed light on the motives that define Big Active.

As a studio we have always had faith in the creative possibilities born out of a spirit of creative collaboration. This instinctive desire stimulates our passion for design and commercial art. We aim to produce seductive and accessible design, and we believe this should work in a way that demands to be appreciated by the head, heart and hips.

Gerard Saint, Creative Director

Seduction & Hustle

AT THE CORE OF BIG ACTIVE there has always been a resolutely gang-like attitude, albeit defined by the hearts of like-minded individuals. The London-based studio was formed in 1990, and developed a belief in creative collaboration that was to set the blueprint for its evolution during the years that followed. Today, the distinctively spirited output of the art direction and design team is uniquely complimented by the success of Big Active's collective group of commercial artists and photographers. It is these creative conspirators who define the wider collaborative picture of Big Active.

Founding partners Gerard Saint, Mark Watkins and Paul Hetherington studied design at Berkshire College of Art, where they shared an interest in music, partying and contemporary graphics. Saint's original plan had been to use the college environment to get a band together, but a growing interest in graphic design and

visual culture provided the perfect alternative distraction. "At the time the immediacy of seeing your work in print just felt much more glamorous than sweating it out in dark rehearsal studios."

After graduating, their paths crossed again in London, and they set upon a plan to make the most of their post-college optimism. Inspired by what they imagined to be the spirit of Push Pin Studios in late-'60s New York, they decided to form a studio to create bold, spirited graphic design, produced with a direct and accessible touch. This new spirit of bravado was to be neatly defined by Hetherington as 'new commercial art'. The name 'Big-Active' was originally allocated to the trio's file by an anonymous official at Companies House when the studio was in the process of being formed. "In the absence of any competing inspiration, it stuck, and we ended up buying the name 'off the shelf' (though we did later delete the hyphen).

Seemingly nonsensical, it could have been a great name for a band, or a brand of sex toys or contraceptives – but best of all it didn't sound like anything to do with the business of design." In retrospect the name has come to perfectly define an attitude of inspired irreverence that has been evident throughout the studio's existence.

Early business cards were printed with 'Fuck Off' on the reverse. "Clients and photocopier salesmen found them amusing, or so we thought." Not every idea saw the light of day, however. An impertinent promotional brochure with the working title of Spunk was to be printed using only mixtures of spot UV varnishes. This plan was sadly shelved due to the pressing need to pay the rent on the studio.

Early work began to grow in the form of commissions from arts organisations, galleries, clothing brands and advertising clients. One such gallery space actually sacked the studio

**Sweet Dreams, Rock, Forever
Promotion, 1999**
A random triptych of posters to
promote the original Big Active
website featuring the rainbow
image. The message could
work in any sequence, or as
individual statements. This is
one of the earliest uses of the
'boy & girl' icon, which was
later redrawn.

A Piece Of Rough, 1994
'John' was a lovable brute
of a barman, working at
the time in a rough and
ready pub on Portobello
Road in west London.
Recognising him as a
'wolf-whistling likely lad',
John was cast first in a
series using regular
people as unlikely icons.
This portrait was shot by
Jocelyn Bain Hogg.

ART-DIRECTION:
BIG-ACTIVE
PHOTOGRAPHY:
JOCELYN BAIN-HOGG
DONKEY JACKET
MODELLED BY
JOHN @ FINCH'S
LONDON W11

ACTIVE

ANOTHER BIG-ACTIVE DESIGN
LONDON 702 9365

High Visibility Art-Direction & Graphic Design. For the Stars of Tomorrow...

after its artists complained that the graphic design was upstaging its exhibitors. "We later realised that design works better sometimes when it's invisible." Big Active spent its formative years learning the business through trial and error. "We were confidently optimistic, but didn't really operate to a prescribed business plan. We were just making it up as we went along – and that's what made it fun and impulsive."

In 1993 a chance meeting with the creators of the newly formed Dazed and Confused led to Big Active's first collaborative art direction role in the shape of an experimental launch of Another magazine. The project lasted three issues, but eventually ran dry after the sponsorship money was exhausted on mounting print bills. "It was an incredibly creative period, and at the time the naïve energy of the experience opened up the possibilities of thinking outside the box of pure graphic design – something we'd always been

drawn towards. Collaboration allowed us to work on bigger ideas, with people whose creative and optimistic irreverence we shared."

During this time the studio also began to take a greater interest in designing for the music industry. The creative buzz around the emerging 'Brit-pop' scene, coupled with a handful of early commissions from the now defunct major labels MCA and Phonogram, provided the catalyst. Here were further kindred souls. "You could turn up to meetings after a heavy night out, and everyone else was in the same state as you. No one batted an eyelid." Jobs were turned around quickly, and the studio learned to thrive on the energy. "It was through MCA that we met Richard Newton, who later joined Big Active to run the management side of things. It was with Richard that we began to explore the possibility of representing a selection of the photographers we regularly worked with on music jobs."

More magazine commissions followed, and in 1996 Saint was asked to art direct a bold new London-based fashion magazine called Scene. "The monthly demands of commissioning gave us an incredible opportunity to work with loads of fresh, up-and-coming photographers and illustrators, as well as more established names like David Bailey. The magazine was visually driven, and this provided us with the freedom to develop a creative team around which we could build a strong identity. We encouraged the use of new illustration to accompany features, and it was through this that we first met Jasper Goodall."

The expedient working structure of Scene also provided the studio with ample oportunities to collaborate conceptually on the magazine's content, and this led to cameo appearances in many of the photo shoots. "I played a pimp in a surveillance story, and a murdered art director in a shot inspired by George Lois," recalls Saint.

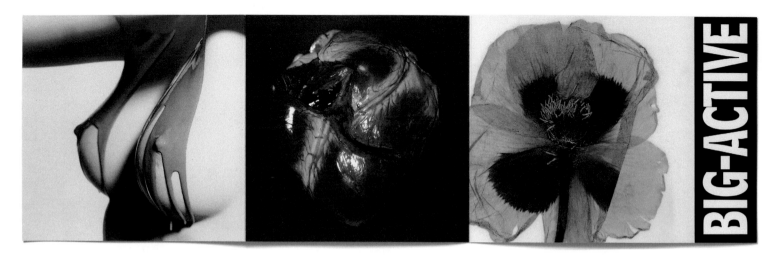

**Chocolate, Hearts & Flowers
Communiqué, 1995**
A concertina-fold valentine
card conceived to bare all the
hallmarks of true romance,
but without the fluff. The
chocolate-covered breasts,
heart and opium poppy were
beautifully shot by Donna
Trope, and mailed out to
arrive on 14th February. Not
everyone was enamoured.
One shrinking violet faxed
back a demand not be sent
any more of this 'awful filth'.

It was during this period that Greg Burne joined
the team. Originally a painter, Burne had come
to Big Active looking for studio space, and was
willing to trade his needs with helping out in the
office. "Greg brought a sense of the working
artist into our design environment, which gave
the studio a whole new dynamic." As things
developed, Burne was to forge a role for himself
as a key player in the studio's drive to cement
relationships with aspiring new image-makers.

In 1997 Hetherington left Big Active to pursue
his own projects, and later to work with Nick
Knight and Peter Saville on their new ShowStudio
venture. "It was time to bring some new vitality to
the studio. We invited WEA's in-house designer,
Mat Maitland, to join the team." Saint had
originally met Maitland during a visit to the label.
"We developed a bond of friendship that has
remained ever since." The designers shared an
interest in music and clubbing, and this led to

many collaborations on music design projects.
"We both had lots of mates who were in bands,
so naturally we'd offer to help out on the design
side of things." Early joint projects included
commissions for Rialto, Lhooq and Republica.

Saint explains, "I'd been really impressed by
Mat's work for bands like Acacia and 808 State,
and I guess we had both wanted to form bands
ourselves at some point, so being part of that
world and designing sleeves together seemed
like the natural thing to do." Maitland's arrival
signalled a turning point for Big Active, and the
studio decided it was time to focus more directly
on the music business. "We hired Mat for his
empathy with music graphics, and his energy
has been a strong influence in developing the
graphic style we are best known for today."

Although much of their work plays with a bold
aesthetic, the team's work is still firmly rooted in
the belief that all great design starts with a

strong and simple idea. "If an idea can't be
articulated simply and successfully over the
phone, it ain't worth a fuck." A sense of intuition
is also important to achieve the desired effect.
"We once designed a CD promo package for a
hedonistic release in the form of a Gucci-styled
luxury 'cocaine kit'. A week after they were sent
out to press and radio, the packages were
changing hands for upwards of £200."

Mischief is often part of the gameplan, but the
studio places an emphasis on combining this
with an intelligent and articulate approach,
which is particularly apparent in their editorial
and book design. "It's all about producing work
that is appropriate – and not losing sight of the
fact that the driving principle behind any brief is
to communicate as effectively as possible."

Assembling the right team of players is key to
crafting a successful result. "Strong art direction
is all about realising an idea, but equally it's

Gerard Saint (Big Active)

Big Active. Design and Art Direction.
Warehouse D4, Metropolitan Wharf, Wapping Wall, London, E1W 3SS.
Tel: +44 (0) 20 7702 9365. Fax: +44 (0) 20 7702 9366. E-mail: gez@bigactive.com
Web: www.bigactive.com

Mat Maitland (Big Active)

Big Active. Design and Art Direction.
Warehouse D4, Metropolitan Wharf, Wapping Wall, London, E1W 3SS.
Tel: +44 (0) 20 7702 9365. Fax: +44 (0) 20 7702 9366. E-mail: m@bigactive.com
Web: www.bigactive.com

Corporate Hostility
Brandalism, 2001
Using Arnie and Jacko as brand-friendly icons of mainstream popular culture, these calling cards aimed to ridicule the intentions of those organisations who are seduced by omnipotent corporate sponsorship. The card on the left was signed by the late and much lamented Clash frontman Joe Strummer.

**Magpies & Blue Tits
Promotion, 2002**
The magpie is a symbol
of the scavaging hoarder,
seduced by the glitter of
shimmering jewels. This
could loosely serve as a
romantic metaphor of the
Big Active aesthetic. The
image was created as
part of a series, playing
with the studio's logo
silhouetted into the sky
over a garden of delights.

We Can Be Heroes
Editorial, 2001
Continuing a theme of unmasking the vice of celebrity, these images were produced for IdN Magazine in Hong Kong. Assuming the characters of Harrison Ford, Pavarotti, Jack Nicholson, JFK, Batman and Kiss frontman Gene Simmons, the Big Active team all feature in this parody of the showman falling for assorted carnal desires.

about allowing enough scope for collaboration to really add an extra dimension." The choice of collaborator is vital. "It's like producing a song and giving it a distinctive sound." This is a requirement, not an indulgence. "We don't go in for that twenty-five-minute drum or guitar solo type of nonsense. Visually, we prefer the short, sharp shock of a three-minute pop classic."

Examples of this collaborative synergy can be seen in much of the studio's output. "One of our first design projects with Jasper Goodall was for a Chicago band called The Webb Brothers, whose legendary father Jimmy Webb wrote the classic Rhinestone Cowboy." When Saint and Maitland invited Goodall to work with them on the campaign, they developed a look that matched Maitland's intuitive typography with Goodall's seductive artwork. "The combination seemed perfectly suited to the image the Webbs were looking to portray."

As the music work grew, so too did the magazine commissions. Saint art directed the relaunch of Nova and notably the award-winning redesign of Viewpoint, a luxe journal forecasting ideas and trends. "Although Nova was short-lived it provided a great vehicle for working with some of the biggest names in fashion and photography."

An increasing turnover of commissioning work, coupled with the development of the seeds of a photographic agency, led to the decision that commercial representation might bring a useful alter ego to the studio. With a roster of photographers already signed up, Greg Burne recognised it was time to develop closer working relationships with illustrators. "At first I wasn't sure that illustration was a market worth pursuing, but when I saw how Jasper worked, I recognised the potential. It was an opportunity to develop a new side to the business."

The studio's reputation was soon attracting the interest of more illustrators. Silkscreen artist Kate Gibb was next to join, swiftly followed by David Foldvari. Although still studying at the RCA, Foldvari was already in demand. "His tutors used to get really pissed off because Dave was already working on big commercial commissions for Nike – possibly there was some frustration involved because he was getting so well paid."

In 2001 Watkins left the group to form his own studio. "In a lot of ways Mark's departure brought the whole idea of operating as a wider creative umbrella into clear perspective." Wearing the badge of creative director, Saint realised it was important for Big Active to take stock of the studio's experience and focus on the future. "Essentially we'd evolved into a creative design studio uniquely working with and representing a collective group of affiliated artists. And that felt like something we could build on."

Big Active Forever, 2002
Jasper Goodall illustrated this image of Greg Burne, Mat Maitland, Gerard Saint and Richard Newton. "We liked the idea of doing something that felt more akin to a shot of a band line-up."

Boy and Girl, Dressed in Pink Lilies, 2004
The silhouette of two lovers embracing first appeared in 1998, and has since undergone a variety of transitions. "A passionate state of pleasure is a beautiful place to be."

Later that year Shiv and Simon Henwood came on board. Simon in particular brought with him an artist's energy combined with a focused sense of commercial enterprise. Having published magazines including Purr and Alice during the 1990s, Henwood was exploring the world of animated features and music video, as well as making the time to paint and exhibit internationally. "It's incredibly important for creators to see themselves in the context of a wide commercial scene. You cannot breathe inside a vacuum." Big Active was by now consolidating its position as a contender at the forefront of new British illustration.

With the collective roster growing, the design studio was earning a respectable reputation for powerful sleeve design with highly visible work for bands including Basement Jaxx and Simian. "We based our Simian campaign around artist Thomas Grünfeld's fantastical cast of disturbing misfit creatures." René Habermacher, who would later be represented by the studio, created the airbrush images that Maitland defaced for the Basement Jaxx campaign. The increasing workload meant it was time to add a new designer to the team. Richard Andrews had been working in-house at BMG Records and had won many awards for his design work for The Cooper Temple Clause. "We'd heard whispers that Rich wanted to move to an independent studio, so we thought, let's go for it."

Photography has played an important role in the work of the studio. "As art directors we have always enjoyed strong creative relationships with a number of fantastic photographers, either collaborating on sleeve designs or commissions for magazines." This has led to book design projects for photographers including Jocelyn Bain Hogg, Deirdre O'Callaghan and David Bailey. "The books have given us an opportunity to get beneath bodies of work, directing them in much the same way a music producer crafts an album."

New photographers too have been attracted to join the group, nurtured under the guidance of Bianca Redgrave. "Photography involves a greater element of production and management. The development and needs of photographers differ greatly from those of the other artists." Whilst Daniel Stier is based in London, many of the Big Active photographers are based outside the UK. Partrick Ibanez and Erwan Frotin in Paris, René Habermacher and Jannis Tsipoulanis in Berlin, and Vava Ribeiro in New York. "Like the artists, each photographer has a distinctive signature style. An individual voice is incredibly important." Expanding this area further, the studio was recently joined by the innovative set director and photographer Rachel Thomas.

Where appropriate, it is natural for the artists to collaborate on projects with the designers in the studio and vice-versa. "It's all about creating a culture that encourages cross-pollination of styles, themes, skills and ideas."

Don't Look The Other Way

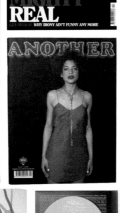
MIGHTY
REAL

ANOTHER

THE WEBB BROTHERS
SUMMER PEOPLE

Goldfrapp

BASEMENT JAXX
Get Me Off

THE FUTUREHEADS

scene

Annie
Chewing Gum

WHO THE FUCK IS BILLY BYRNE?
TOMORROW YOUR LIFE WILL CHANGE. I HOPE YOU'RE READY

Ladytron
Seventeen

viewpoint
#9
FEAR UNCERTAINTY & DOUBT

ATHLETE

Goldfrapp

STRICT MACHINE

simian
chemistry is what we are
(lp)

simian mobile disco.

THE LAST MINUTE

Ed Harcourt
All Of Your Days Will Be Blessed

BASEMENT JAXX
ROMEO

Ladytron

RIALTO
DREAM ANOTHER DREAM.

SIMIAN
NEVER BE ALONE

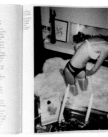

DESERT EAGLE DISCS FEAT. KEISHA WHITE
BIGGER BETTER DEAL

SHY FX & T POWER/FEELIN' U
FEATURING KELE LE ROC

PAUL THEROUX

I AM KLOOT

BASEMENT JAXX
UNDER FIRE

KINESIS
BILLBOARD BEAUTY

WHERE'S YOUR HEAD AT

YOU NEED ME

simian
the wisp
(lp)

Jus 1 Kiss

VIOLENT DELISH

SOMETHING'S GOING ON

SPAN

THE KENNEDY

Product of God
Identity, 2004
The magpie metaphor
was revisited to create
the identity for Big Active's
range of limited edition
large format artists' prints.
"We thought we'd make
our bird a bit cuter and
bolder as a nod to the
iconic heritage of the
puffin and penguin."

ProductOfGod

This philosophy is key to understanding the working methods of Big Active, and it is one that has been driven by the design team, keen to explore new visual routes. "Our primary objective is to represent artists in the wider commercial market, but we also encourage a cross-feed with our own team on relevant design projects."

This collaborative climate encourages both art director and artist to work closely, and throws up the possibility of discovering unforeseen routes. "There is no reason why an artist should not explore the possibilities of design. Creativity must be democratic, it's simply a case of ideas and direction." The broad scope of opportunities often means that individual artists have the chance to try out new ideas and develop their voices in new areas. Jasper Goodall is currently working on a brand of deluxe bikinis with swimwear designer Louise Middleton, and Mat Maitland

continues to develop his distinctive photomontage style by borrowing from an ever-expanding range of inspirational sources.

As the creative network grows, Big Active has learned to cultivate an atmosphere that is aware of the demands of the marketplace and the need for a showcase that can continually be reinvigorated and respond successfully to change. In 2004 Kristian Russell, Kam Tang, Will Sweeney and Geneviève Gauckler all joined, bringing with them an energetic mix of styles and disciplines. With a wide array of visual approaches to tap into, the team has the flexibility to view any new commission from a variety of angles. An external network of creatives, a focused in-studio resource, and a decade and a half's experience of pushing the envelope to explore new design solutions, all combine to ensure the creative juices continue to flow with calculated abandon.

Big Active tries to encourage a youthfulness of spirit, but one that is constantly maturing and evolving, making way for new energy and influence whilst capitalising on accumulated reputation and experience. Saint believes that being able to constantly reinvent and invigorate is a vital ingredient for the success of the studio. For that reason, the team will always be on the look-out for fresh collaborators. "Commercial art is about communicating in a seductive and memorable way, and it is this provocation which feeds our desire to embrace new talent."

In acknowledging the need to adapt and move forward when considering new artists, Burne detects an important shift in perception. "I think the nature of commercial art and graphics has changed. Illustrators can now have star profiles, just like photographers – it's all about producing imagery that's both pertinent and captivating."

**Her Majesty's Pleasure
Spring/summer 2003**
In a spontaneous act of
reverie this promotional
T-shirt graphic was created
by David Foldvari on the
back of an old envelope.

"We have always believed in a creative approach that embraces a sense of collaboration. Concept and direction are our primary concerns, with the aim being to find a balance where design and image-making can come together seamlessly."

Basement Jaxx/Rooty Album campaign, 2001
The band's early demos for the album were charged with an electric sexual tension. We initially suggested producing a series of kitsch 80s-style airbrush images of sexy girls, which could later be naïvely defaced, as the basis for the style of the campaign. The Jaxx's Felix Buxton was at our studio one day, fresh from a holiday in Spain, and pulled out a postcard of Snowflake, the albino gorilla who was the main attraction at Barcelona zoo. We all thought he would make a great cover star for the album sleeve. Building on that thought, we proposed creating an imaginary zoo, which would allow us to feature different animals on each of the single covers. The concept was promptly approved, so we asked airbrush artist René Habermacher to illustrate Snowflake and his band of imaginary friends. Later Mat Maitland colluded with graffiti artist Rob Kidney to deface the slick pictures and finalise the sleeve designs. As the campaign developed it came full circle. Although our intial intention was to continue the zoo theme, the raw sexual energy of the single Get Me Off somehow demanded a human pin-up. Luckily we were able to find a model whose animal instincts were suitably untamed. Snowflake was to enjoy new fame as an icon for one of the UK's finest dance acts, before sadly passing away in 2003.

Goldfrapp/Black Cherry Album campaign, 2003
Classic children's stories and burlesque Berlin cabaret are two of the multistranded themes behind the imagery for Alison Goldfrapp's Black Cherry album campaign. Alison's original vision was for an illusive world of tantalising innocence reborn as sparkling adult fantasy. Cues were taken from sources as diverse as Grimm's fairytales and archive Ladybird nursery books – but revisited via the dark fog of adolescent perspective. Alison was keen for the final imagery to have a rough, uneven, handcrafted look, which we agreed would lend a spontaneous dynamic to the overall mood. To create the basic source material, we asked Polly Borland to

photograph Alison at an run-down stately home near London. In scripting the shoot, we dreamt up a Little Red Riding-Hood scenario with an urgent sexual undertone. Stylist Fi Jones dressed this up for us with decadent grandeur, mixed together with Freudian whispers of childhood reverie. The shoot took place on a chilly autumn day, with a pack of friendly huskies standing in as their Big, Bad cousins. The faded opulence of the house lent a haunting, oppressive air, that was captured in Polly's beautiful and possessed pictures. After the final edit Mat Maitland got to work on the prints with a pair of blunt-edged scissors to produce the collages that became synonymous with the music.

**Span/Mass Distraction
Album, 2003**

If you've ever wanted to experience the adulation and devoted worship of adoring fans, please pause for the next thirty seconds to consider this spread. As you make out individual characters in the sea of faces, you will begin to notice a more sinister side. Lurking in the shadows are your devils and nightmares, staring right back at you. Mass Distraction is the Gil Norton-produced debut album by Norwegian rockers Span. We really liked the idea of doing something stripped back and direct in feel. Imagery that used the power of the graphic statement rather than flashy production or print techniques. Right from the start we ruled out simply putting the band on the cover, so we thought it would be amusing to throw the spotlight on the fans. Collaborating with Big Active artist David Foldvari, we envisaged the idea of creating a vast crowd scene. As 'Mass Distraction' suggests, the collective voice of the crowd is defined by its individual personalities. And we wanted plenty of those. A competition was launched on the bands' website to search for faces. The crowd scene was designed to extend out from the front cover across a six-panel roll-fold booklet printed in one colour. Keen observers will spot each of the band members, spread out among their crew, friends, freaks and demons – and the faces of Big Active.

FutureLoopFoundation/ Scratch & Sniff, 2004

Futureloop (Mark Barrott) asked us to produce a special package for his summer 2004 EP project. Mark wanted this release to appear only in a 10" vinyl format, available from a select number of outlets. He believed that the sleeve could become an integral part of the release, completing the experience. The EP and individual tracks were all untitled at the outset, which allowed us to explore together the many organic possibilities arising from a truly collaborative design process. We discussed ideas of summertime and the warm feelings awoken within. Mat Maitland and Big Active artist Jasper Goodall developed two visuals that conjured up memories of unsullied childhood summers. We then wanted to enhance the effect by impregnating key areas of the images with silk-screen printed aromas of freshly mown grass, vanilla ice cream and bubble gum – to add to the sensory ambience of summer vibes. After an anxious check to ensure the desired flavours were available, the package was complete. For extra lustre, the sleeves were printed in fluorescent inks, and the type applied with silver foil blocking. There's no front and back as such, allowing the two images to be displayed together for racking. Finally, the text on the inner sleeve was printed white out of solid fluorescent yellow, to mimic the effect of staring directly into the sun.

Aloud by Aloud
Album campaign, 2004
Parisian dance duo Aloud requested sun-kissed fantasies, trashy rock and roll dreams and hot beach party action. We set about delivering a campaign narrative that would fulfil the brief, but add a twist of the unexpected. We finally decided to focus on the exploits of a gate-crashing groupie with an agenda all her own. Inspired by the work of Allen Jones and Philip Castle for Pirelli in the 70s, we wanted to give the images a feeling of exaggerated sexual empowerment. We called upon Big Active artist Shiv to bring this 'ligger with attitude' to life. Her edgy illustrations added a sense of danger and seduction, along with a self-confident glamour. Our groupie sets about tempting the band with illusions of sex and sun, and the promise of hedonistic desire fulfilled. But she ends up trashing the party with the power of provocative suggestion. Booze gets poured over amplifiers, equipment is smashed and recording tape recycled for sadistic bondage games. Not quite the kind of thrash the band had been bargaining for.

**Pleasure by Pleasure
Album, 2003**
Pleasure by Pleasure is the fruit of a collective music project put together by producer, musician and friend of Big Active, Fred Ball. The studio album features guest vocals from a host of eminent recording artists including Justine Frischmann (ex-Elastica), Ed Harcourt and Cerys Matthews. Our own Mat

Maitland co-wrote and sang on a couple of the tracks, as well as designing the visuals. Calling upon a wide range of idiosyncratic themes, the resulting collage explores a fantasy utopia of delights, recreations and desires. Capitalising on his new-found narcissism, Mat included his own image on the cover. That's him staring out from the visor.

14. October. 2004. London

BobSeger

V.Pop '2004
14.10-LONDON

Jasper Goodall
René Habermacher
& Jannis Tsipoulanis
Kate Gibb
Vava Ribeiro
Shiv
Erwan Frotin
Kam Tang
David Foldvari
Patrick Ibanez
Geneviève Gauckler
Mat Maitland
Daniel Stier
Kristian Russell
Will Sweeney
Simon Henwood
Rachel Thomas

Jasper Goodall

"I have an ongoing fascination," says Jasper Goodall, "with trying to decode why I like a piece of artwork, be it my own or someone else's." He describes this indefinable quality as something that causes a 'desire reaction', whether it be in art or commercial illustration. "I try through my artwork to press people's desire buttons – I'm not sure where they are, but I try to push them." Jasper's influences are eclectic, from Aubrey Beardsley, to 70s' illustration and design, to fashion photographers like Helmut Newton. "I also take facets from more traditional craft-based areas like Japanese print, Indian Batik or natural history illustration and use them as I see fit.

"My work is very utopian, it's about desires and fantasies. I am never really sure how a piece of work will turn out when I start it; it just kind of takes shape. The end result is the most satisfying. Looking at a finished piece of work provides the excitement and fuels the passion to continue creating." Once personally satisfied, he is keen to explore the audience response. "I am aware of the apparent divisions placed between art and illustration. My real desire is to create artwork that people enjoy solely as art, not just as a selling tool. What I am trying to do is break down the barriers. I want to be allowed to create are an amalgam and distillation of women from fashion, glamour and a surrogate form of photography that, if time and budget were no object, I might

His reccurring interest lies in the beauty and sexual power of women. "The women I create are an amalgam and distillation of women from fashion, glamour and pornography. I will chop up existing photographs and assemble, like Frankenstein, the model that I want, doing what I want her to be doing. I create the imagery through a surrogate form of photography that, if time and budget were no object, I might

employ as a process." To attain the image he has in his mind, he uses colour and shape to fill in the gaps. He is unambiguous about portraying sexual desire. "We all have sexual fantasies, some more 'out there' than others. I think people get turned on by looking at sexual imagery but are too embarrassed to admit it. I like to push the audience a little. Sexual illustration is an area where this can be explored." The situations he concocts are inspired by his imagination, and Jasper is quick to assert that "no one was really there, doing what is depicted." He believes that viewers who feel comfortable with their desires will not find such images offensive. "Context helps. Having sexual work in an art arena moves it away from the taboo of the porn mag or the sex shop." He suggests though, "It's harder on a personal level to present this kind of work because it's entirely from one's own mind, and therefore says something about the individual who made it."

Jasper recognises that photographic pornography is often too gritty, imperfect and not very beautiful – just the same images regurgitated over and over again. "What turns me on is akin to a journey, it is very much dependent on mood. You can be very surprised about what stimulates you. I am constantly surprised at the way people do not push their passions and desires and shy away from being honest about what it is that turns them on." He believes there is a sliding scale between pornographic imagery at one end and art at the other. "I feel sexual desire and appreciation of art perhaps come from the same place in the mind. Both are valid forms of expression, and both can be used to appreciate the image."

Aphrodite

Goddess of Love and Passion

Psyche&Eros

The union of Heart and Mind

Persephone&Hades

The daughter of Demeter and her captor, Lord of the Underworld

Leda&TheSwan

Zeus seduces the nymph Leda in the guise of a swan

Bacchus

God of Wine and Excess

TheFuries

Torturers and Tormentors

Ares&Aphrodite

Aphrodite's favourite among her many lovers was Ares, God of War and Aggression

René Habermacher & Jannis Tsipoulanis

The work of René Habermacher and Jannis Tsipoulanis is a captivating synthesis of elegance and artifice. "What we try to do is achieve perfection in the images we create." Their photographic source material is pushed into the realm of the hyper-real, as they seek to refine traditional concepts of beauty. "We have a deep interest and regard for the classical Greek period, which relied heavily on realism but also a perfection that has not been achieved since. What we are looking to express is very much grounded in our way of perceiving the world and our influences. We want to convey strength and eroticism. The technique is not about retouching; it's about destroying and building something from nothing. The end result shows everything in its minutest detail, which retouching seeks to obliterate."

Their approach delivers a heightened sense of desire and luxury. "We have been surprised by the response this work has engendered. It seems we have captured a moment at present. There is no understatement in the images we create. The fashion where this style of work is being sought out. Glamour plays a significant role in fashion at present. There is no understatement in the images we create. The computer has made the realisation of this work easier and faster." Building an image can be freeform, intuitive. "You can do whatever you want with it. Sometimes we have no idea where it will lead." But the final work must be underpinned by thought and meaning. "Working together is a battlefield, but we both have the same vision. It is our common interests that bring everything together."

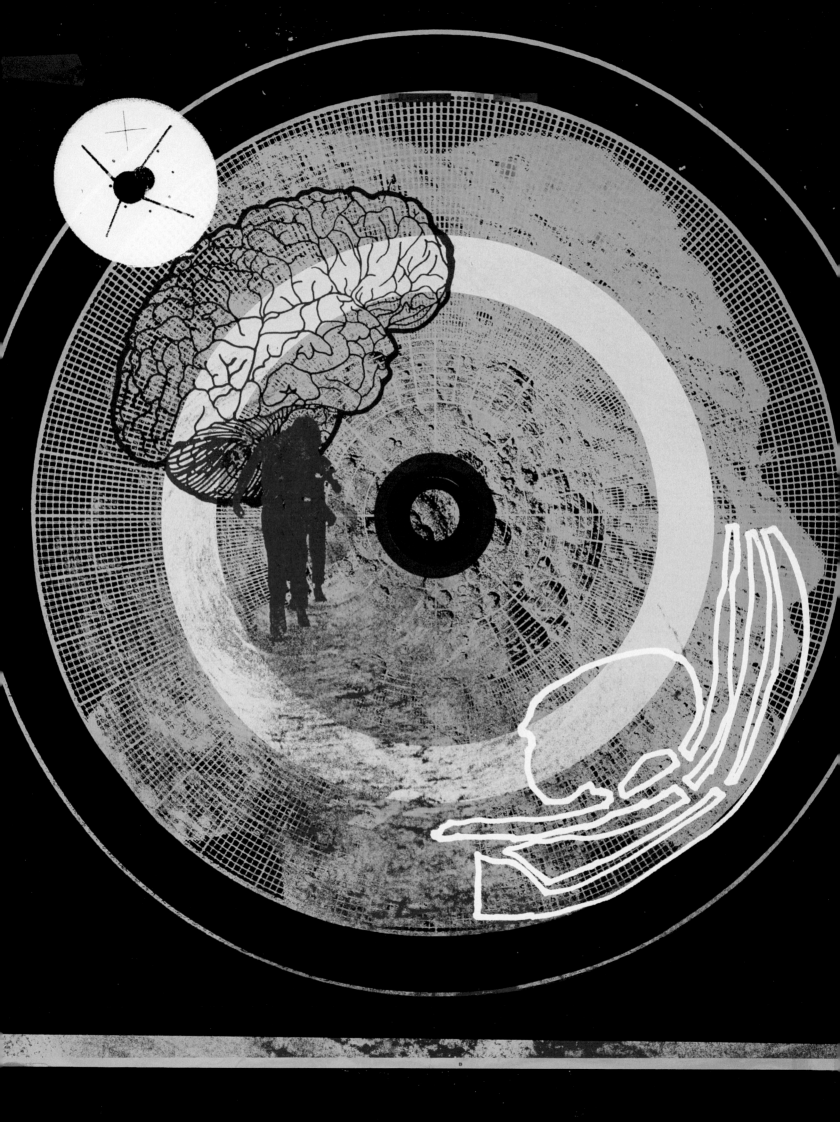

Kate Gibb

The work of Kate Gibb always has to be understood within the context of the process of screen printing. "I always describe myself as a screen printer and not an illustrator or artist. I am influenced by my surroundings, what I experience in my everyday life, something I might see on the way to work, an image in a newspaper, a comment overheard. "The elements in her work come from a mish-mash of sources. Everything from taking pictures, collecting paper-based graphic objects, to looking through old magazines. They all create a collage of inspiration. "I think in pictures and don't write much down. If I find a ticket for instance, it's not just the ticket itself I am inspired by, it's what it reminds me of, the place it was found in. I am thinking about what I am looking at from a possible printing/artwork perspective."

Kate's education included a degree in textiles and this early background is still very much evident in her work and its emphasis on colour. "I am very into colour and mark-making. As my working life has progressed I have learnt so much more about the medium. For me the joy of printing is in the controlled accidents, the layering up of images and colour, discovering and revealing new images as you keep printing. It's never planned. If you know the outcome before you begin you've killed the creativity. The physical process is an integral part of the work."

Consequently Kate has never actively pursued using the computer as part of the creative process. "I like the end result to be something I have made, that I can pick up and hold in my hand. There is a fantastical element to my work, but the very fact that I can do this for a living is the greatest fantasy."

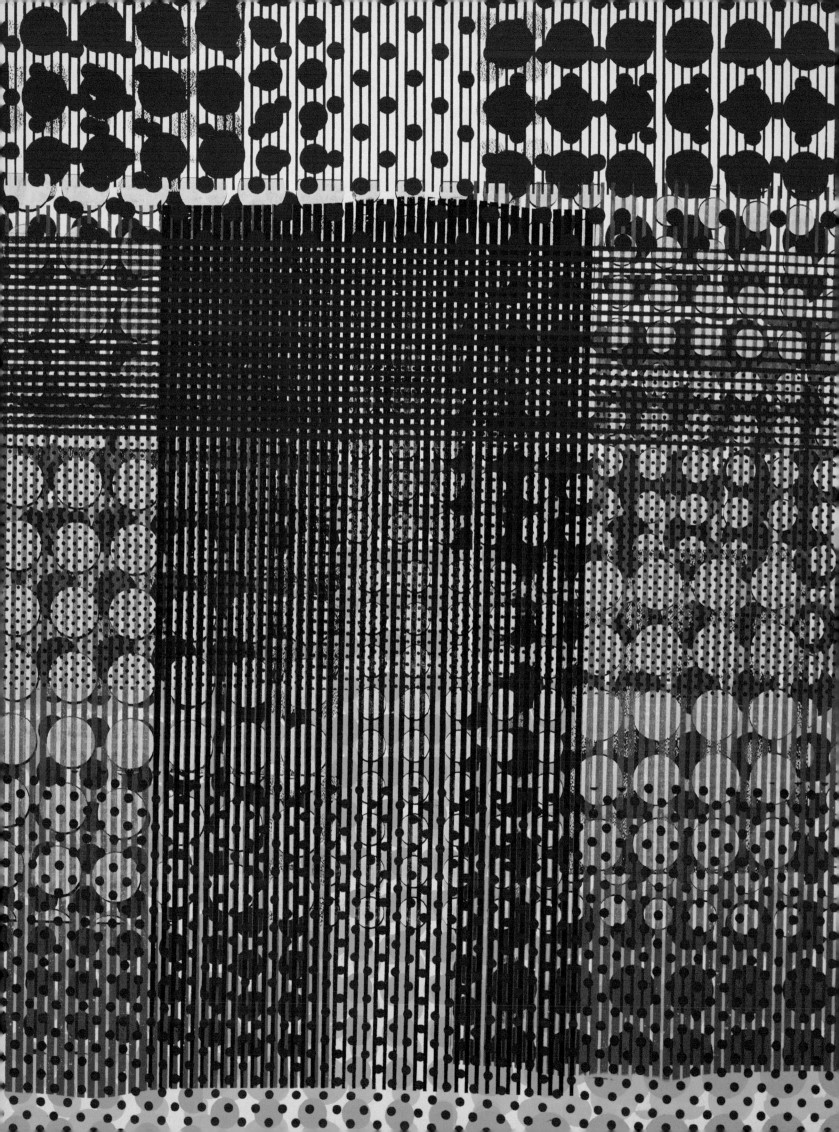

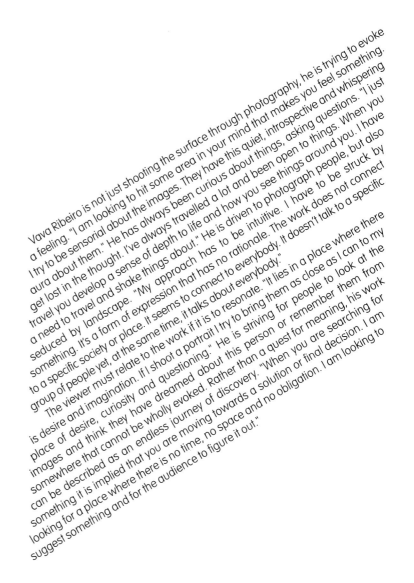

Vava Ribeiro is not just shooting the surface through photography, he is trying to evoke a feeling. "I am looking to hit some area in your mind that makes you feel something. I try to be sensorial about the images. They have this quiet, introspective and whispering aura about them." He has always been curious about things, asking questions. "I just get lost in the thought. I've always travelled a lot and been open to things. When you travel you develop a sense of depth to life and how you see things around you. I have a need to travel and shake things about." He is driven to photograph people, but also seduced by landscape. "My approach has to be intuitive. I have to be struck by something. It's a form of expression that has no rationale. The work does not connect to a specific society or place. It seems to connect to everybody. It doesn't talk to a specific group of people yet, at the same time, it talks about everybody."

The viewer must relate to the work if it is to resonate. "It lies in a place where there is desire and imagination. If I shoot a portrait I try to bring them as close as I can to my place of desire, curiosity and questioning." He is striving for people to look at the images and think they have dreamed about this person or remember them from somewhere that cannot be wholly evoked. Rather than a quest for meaning, his work can be described as an endless journey of discovery. "When you are searching for something it is implied that you are moving towards a solution or final decision. I am looking for a place where there is no time, no space and no obligation. I am looking to suggest something and for the audience to figure it out."

Vava Ribeiro

PAIXO TROPICAL (PASSION FRUIT)
STARRING PAULA GUILLEM WITH BERNARDO AND CAMILA DUBAY

"PAULA WE ARE SO IN SYNC, WE FEEL THE SAME..."
"PAULA AGENTE TA' EM SINTONIA, EU SINTO O MESMO QUE VOCE..."

"...IT'S BECAUSE YOU ARE MY BROTHER!"
"...CLARO, VOCE È MEU IRMÃO!"

"WHEN WE KISS THE WORLD TURNS... BLUE"
"QUANDO EU TE BEIJO O MUNDO FICA... AZUL"

"WHEN WE KISS THE WORLD TURNS... PINK"
"QUANDO EU TE BEIJO O MUNDO FICA... ROSA"

"HE TOLD ME THAT LOVE IS ONLY GOOD WHEN IT HURTS..."
"ELE ME DISSE QUE AMOR SO'E' BOM QUANDO DOI'..."

"... BUT PAIN IS JUST ONE SHADE OF PASSION"
"... MAS A DOR E' APENAS UMA NUANCE DA PAIXO"

"YOU TASTE LIKE A MANGO..."
"VOCE E' DOCE COMO UMA MANGA..."

"... I'M A PINK MANGO IN YOUR MOUTH"
"... EU SOU UMA MANGA ROSA NA SUA BOCA"

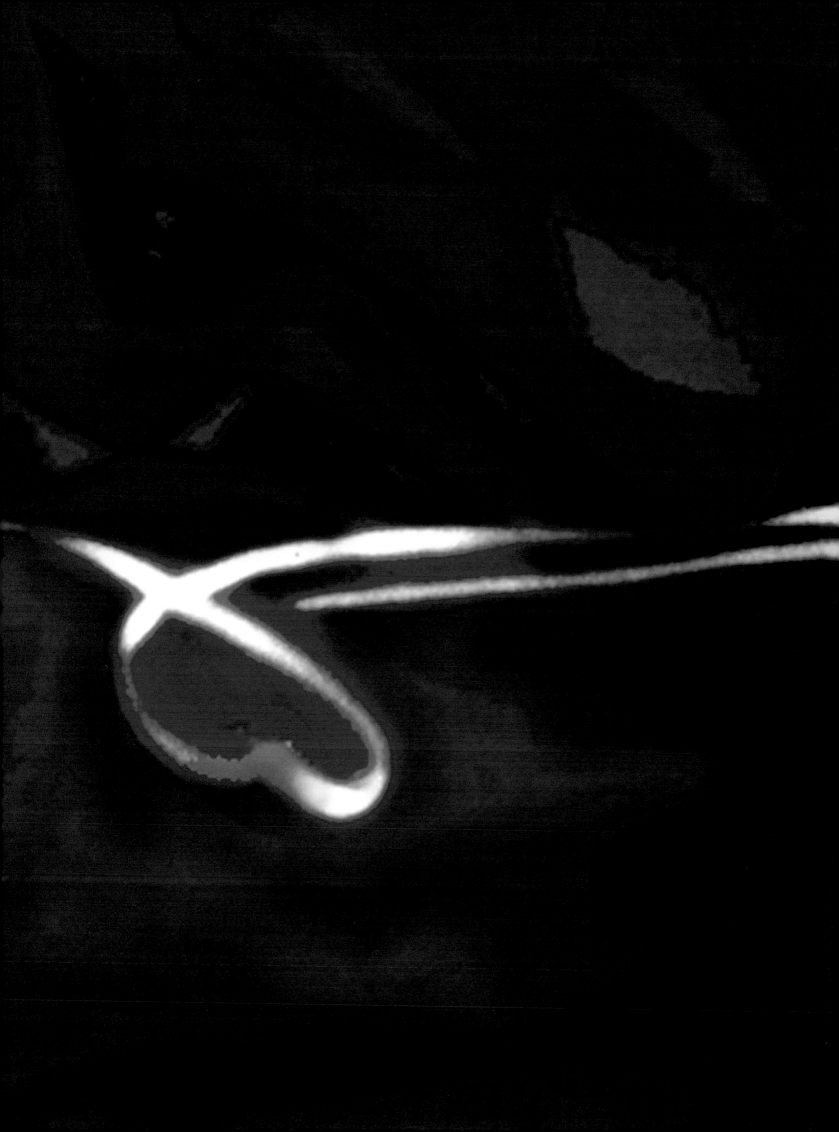

Shiv's work, though illustrative, is much more about channelling ideas into conveying mood or feeling. "It works better when there is ambiguity. How much of a reality is allowed to come through dictates how illustrative, or how abstract, it will be."

Shiv turns to photographers more than other illustrators for influence. "I look to retain an element of the real world and this can be achieved with photography, the starting point for any of the imagery." Her work is built up in many layers, with a view to stripping back to discover the essence. "I am looking to keep a nostalgia of feeling and emotion that you can evoke more with realism. I grew up watching a lot of films and that has fed a need to create a wider landscape to the work and make it more filmic. It's more about creating a scene and not about being abstract. Everything has to appear quite solid."

Music has provided a constant in her work, allowing her to secure a number of sleeve design commissions. It has never been wholly about possessing the music in itself, but more about being part of the creation process for this medium. When she has the opportunity to design a sleeve she wants to create an image that the music can exist in. Clarity of expression is always key. "I want people to stop and really look when they see the work, but not in a way that tries to subvert. I want them to look at the detail. The work is not dark and depressing, and nor does it make huge statements. It's a snapshot of how I look at the world."

Shiv

The style of Erwan Frotin's work is dictated by an organic approach to image-making. It's about conveying growth; selecting and transforming a variety of influences to give life to something new. He has a natural bent for observing small details and collecting them in his mind. "I absorb a lot and spit everything out when I have to do a picture. I have learnt a great deal from the Paris-based studio M/M who were professors of mine. They taught us how to do something personal but, at the same time, something that can be used in commercial work. It's more of a game of playing with shapes, but never revealing myself." Before becoming a photographer he studied medicine and biology. After one year of study he realised it was more of an aesthetic interest. "This period comes back to me through use of shape and a scientific point of view. I try to create something that is humorous but, at the same time, elegant. My pictures can look quite crazy but for me it is serious."

The sensuality in his work comes from the way he arranges the objects. "The arrangements can appear to be clinical but not too cold. I try to put something in that can be quite sexual to balance the clinical." Surrealism has been a formative influence and often resurfaces in the work. "I started to associate things that had nothing in common and try to tell a story and make them live together. I like it when it looks almost perfect but appears to be a work in progress. It comes from an interest in styling the object and making the shapes." For Erwan when it's shot, it's finished; he doesn't want to see the images anymore. "It's part of this natural feeling I want to show in the work. I prefer and am happiest in the assembling of the object. I look to create something in between masculine and feminine. I try to be ambiguous yet try and attain a sensual and erotic mood rather than sexual. This relationship is based on their texture and not what they are." He wants to show the familiar in a way that surprises, but doesn't shock. "If I change the point of view of what people already know then it is surprising, more than trying to show something they do not know. Doing small things perfectly is a turn-on for me. In everyday life I am quite clumsy. Shooting still life is the only time when I am so concentrated that I do everything really well."

Erwan Frotin

Kam Tang

Kam Tang grew up on a diet of Marvel comics and, after being taught technical drawing and draughtsmanship at school, decided to study graphic design at college. He didn't start out with the intention of becoming an illustrator, but gradually his interest in drawing took over. "The solutions I came up with were always illustrative and never typographic," he states, though an appreciation of typography is evident throughout his work.

He endeavours to attain a balance between thought and practice, fantasy and reality, contemplation and application. "I start with pen and paper. I try and get everything down on paper to clear my head of any thoughts." Only then can he truly focus on the job in hand. "You need to grasp what is required for any given project, and the angle of view. I like the solitary nature of it. I am not a team player and only want to be responsible for myself." He has to be happy with the work first before others see it. There are media he has not explored and is curious to know how his work would change in other disciplines. The balance between fantasy and reality is always shifting. Nothing can be planned. "I get excited when I know I am taking the work into new territory."

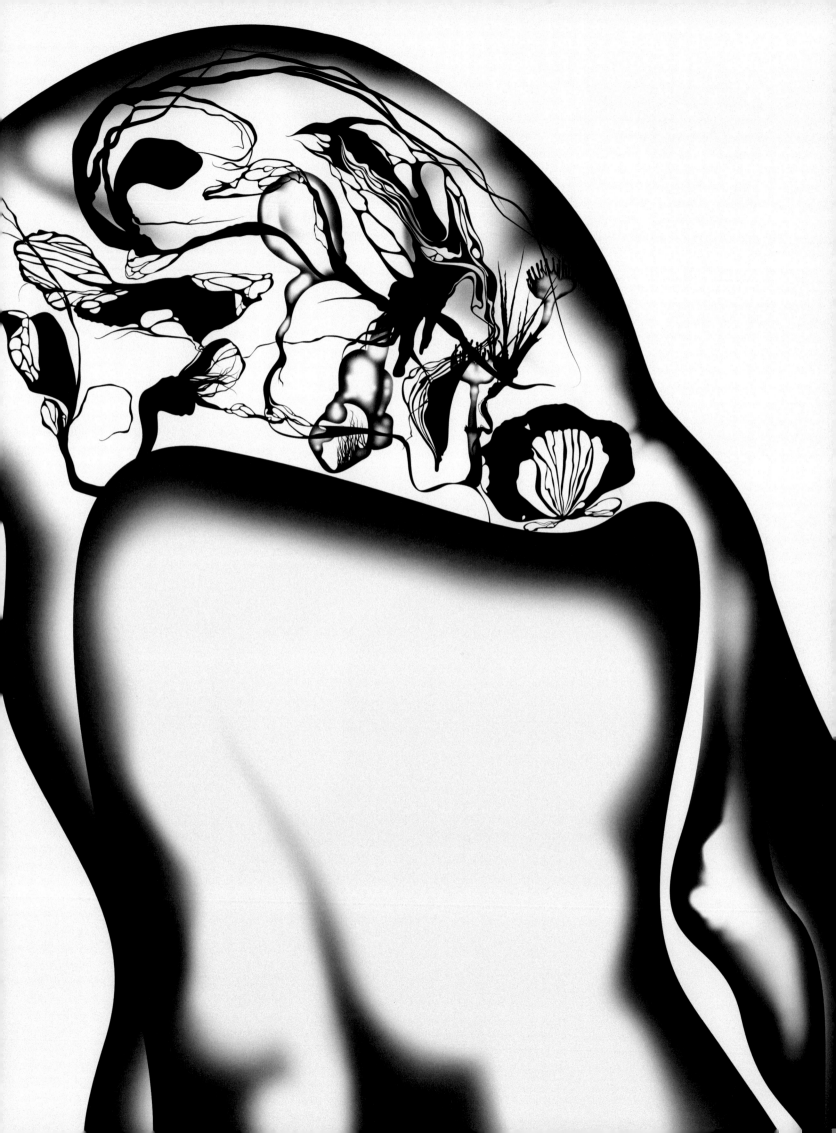

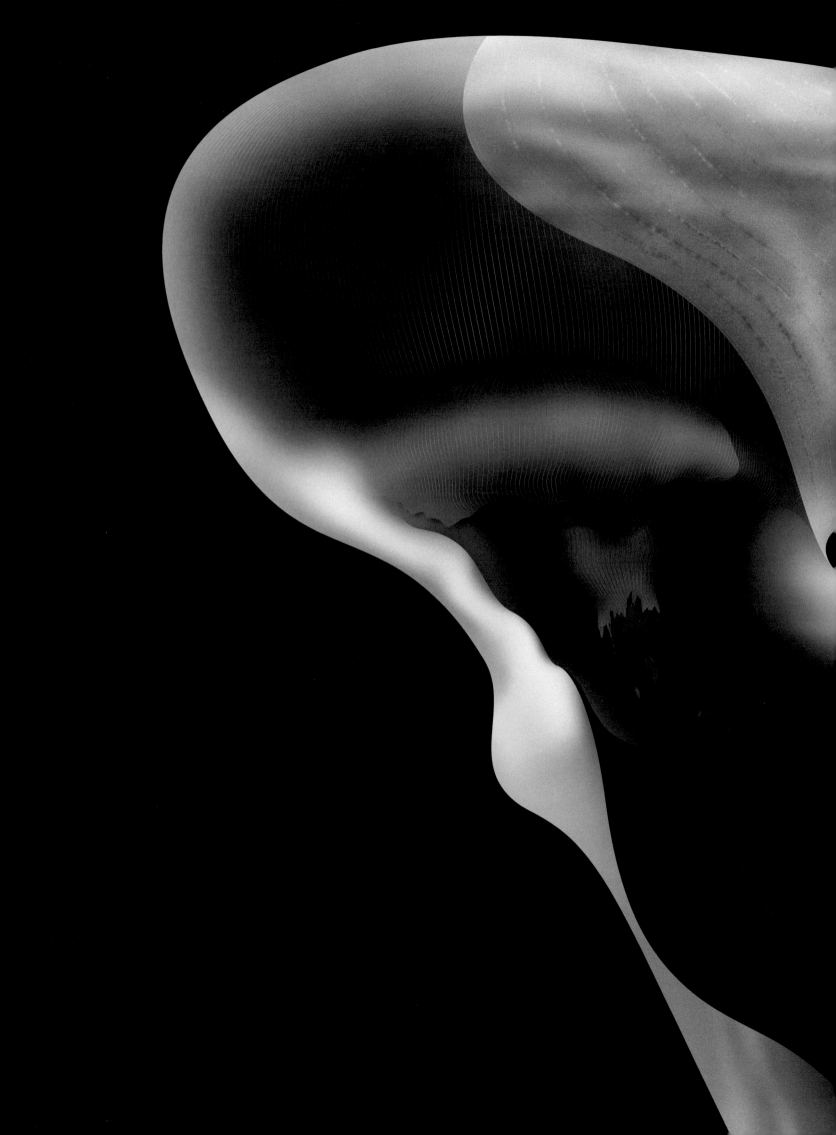

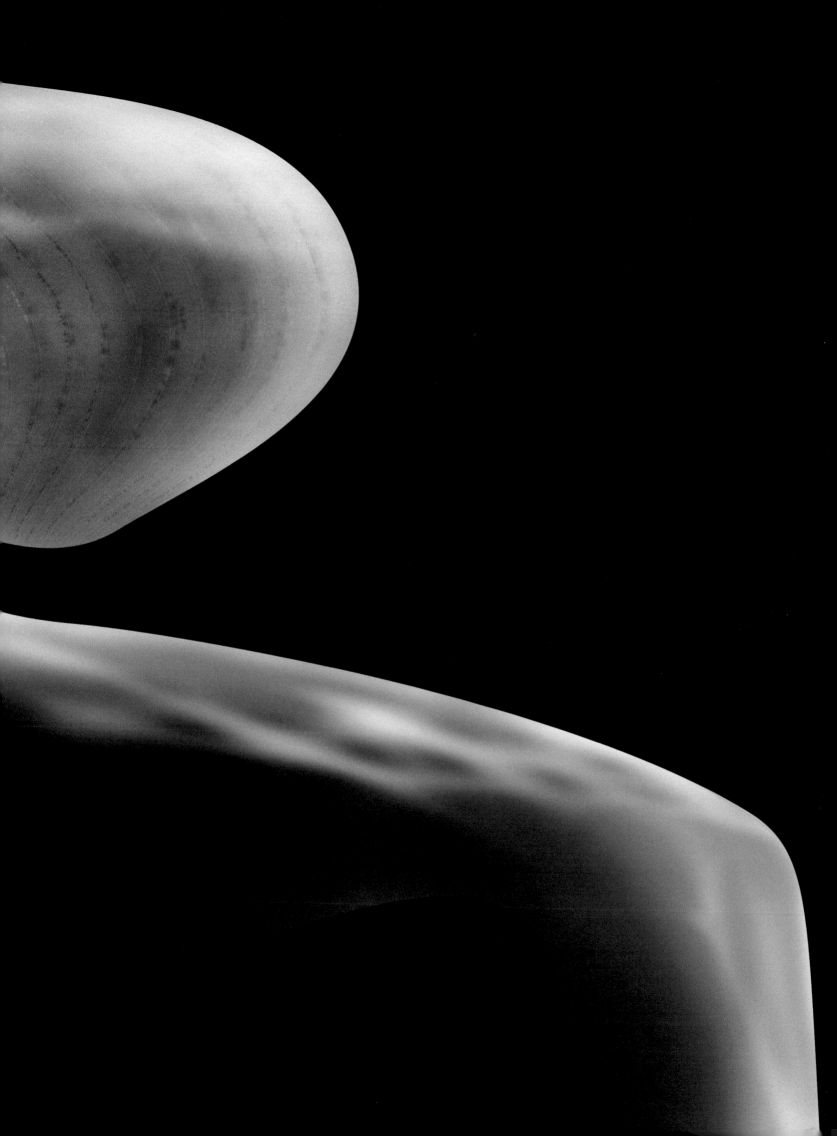

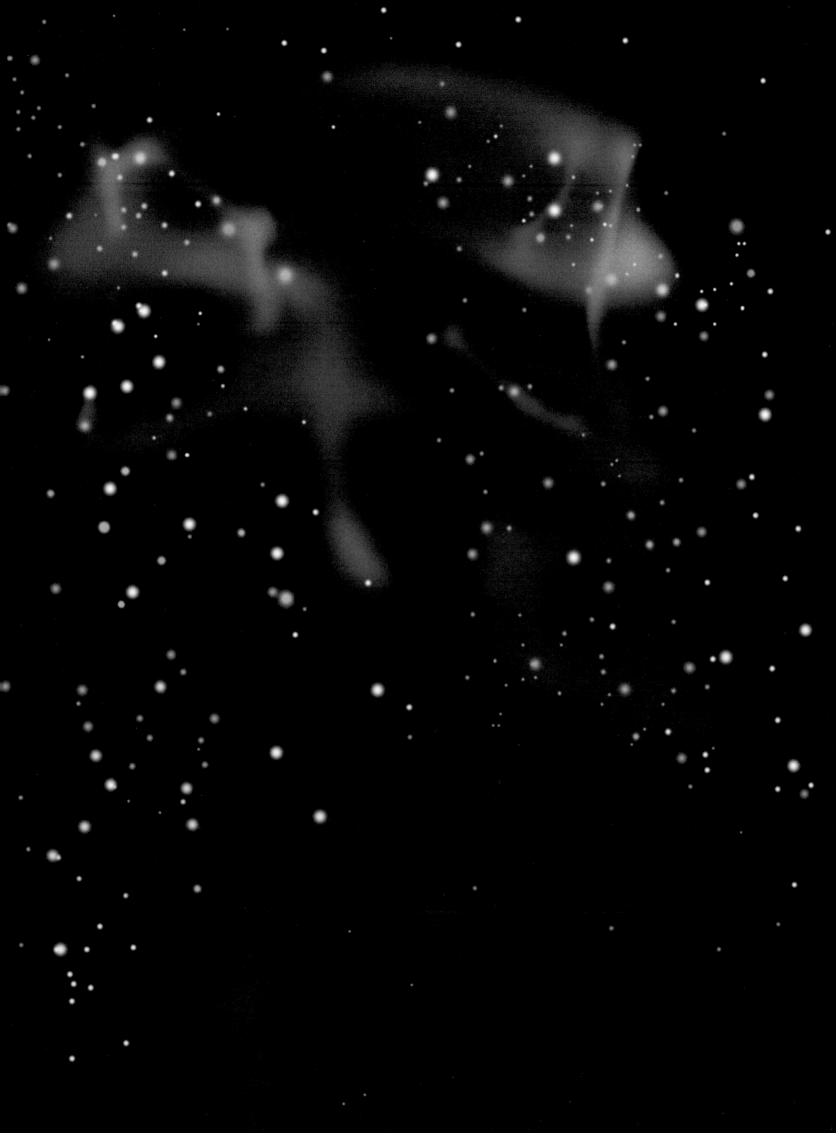

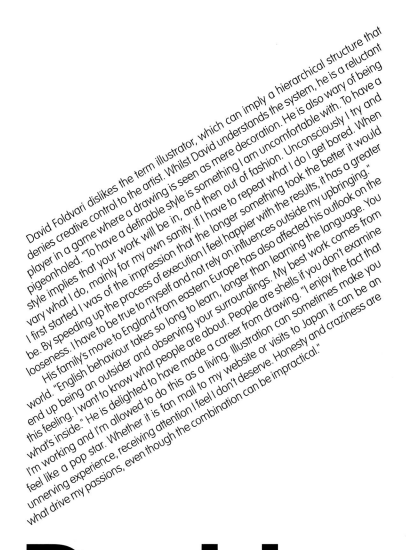

David Foldvari dislikes the term illustrator, which can imply a hierarchical structure that denies creative control to the artist. Whilst David understands the system, he is a reluctant player in a game where a drawing is seen as mere decoration. He is also wary of being pigeonholed. "To have a definable style is something I am uncomfortable with. To have a style implies that your work will be in, and then out of fashion. Unconsciously I try and vary what I do, mainly for my own sanity. If I have to repeat what I do I get bored. When I first started I was of the impression that the longer something took the better it would be. By speeding up the process of execution I feel happier with the results, it has a greater looseness. I have to be true to myself and not rely on influences outside my upbringing."

His family's move to England from eastern Europe has also affected his outlook on the world. "English behaviour takes so long to learn, longer than learning the language. You end up being an outsider and observing your surroundings. My best work comes from this feeling. I want to know what people are about. People are shells if you don't examine what's inside." He is delighted to have made a career from drawing. "I enjoy the fact that I'm working and I'm allowed to do this as a living. Illustration can sometimes make you feel like a pop star. Whether it is fan mail to my website or visits to Japan it can be an unnerving experience, receiving attention I feel I don't deserve. Honesty and craziness are what drive my passions, even though the combination can be impractical."

David Foldvari

Patrick Ibanez

Patrick Ibanez was once in awe of photography. "When I was young, photographers were gods and I thought I would only be able to look at their pictures and never be a photographer myself. When I was doing my military service I met a guy who showed me how easy it was to use a camera. There was no formal training." The learning came in part from trial and error, but chiefly from speaking to photographers, art directors and other professionals, to understand what was needed across a range of commissions. "They gave me opportunities to dream. I was not looking to be a fashion photographer. It was just by accident. What I have learnt is that photography is about working as a team to bring out something that is not apparent." Patrick believes the best photography is, above all else, instinctive. "It's all part of capturing something that is there for a fleeting moment. First of all I am selfish and I go for the things that I like.

"It's about ideas and taste and then a little bit of technique. It has to come directly from your heart. It's all about luck and a need to be surprised, more so by yourself."
The most profound influence on Patrick has been Guy Bourdin, for whom he once worked. "He seemed to have some level of perversity in all aspects of his life, but not in a bad way. If I had stayed within his way of thinking I would never have been capable of working as a photographer. When I left I stopped doing fashion pictures for a year. I looked into other areas of photography. I had to figure out what was there in this work that I could bring to fashion." To Patrick an assignment has to be about excitement and surprise for him to give of his best. "It's about excelling in your work beyond your dreams. The biggest turn-on is to challenge myself, to see how far I can go. I need to know that people trust in me. Without that trust and confidence you make mistakes. You should be left to be free without intrusion."

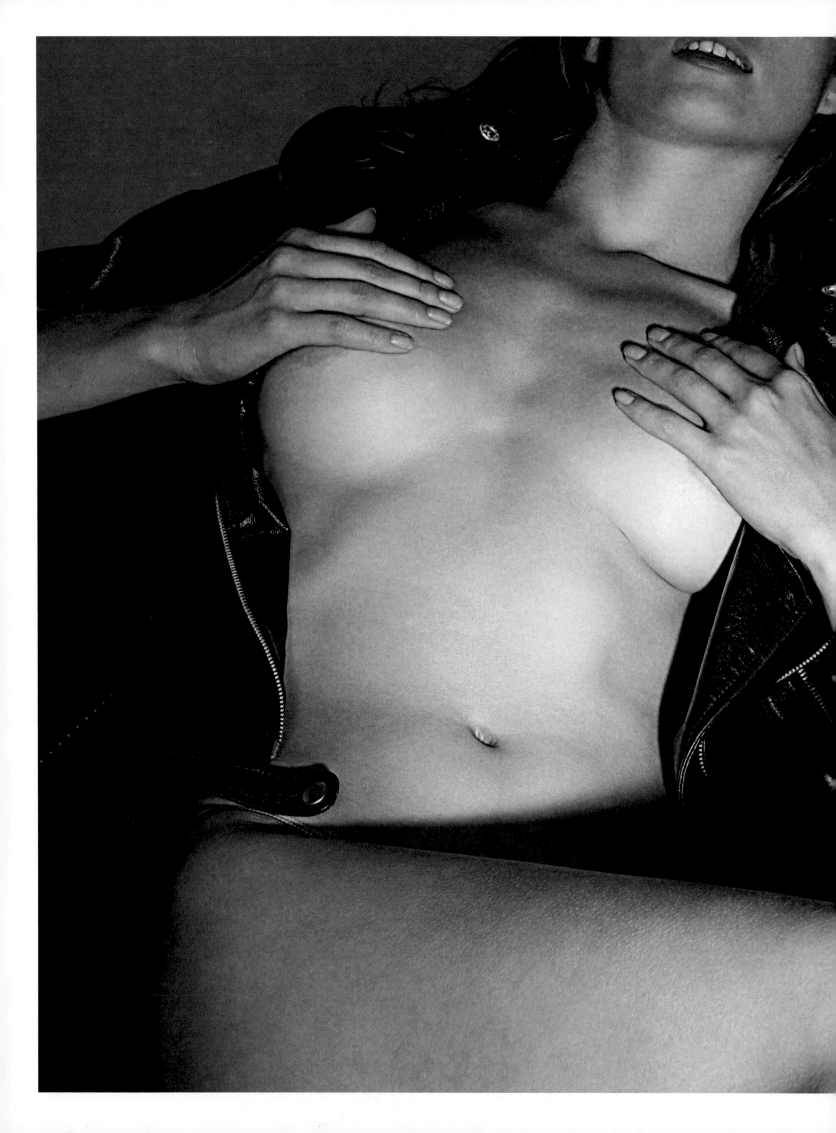

Geneviève Gauckler

Geneviève Gauckler is constantly switching between the differing boundaries and disciplines of graphic design and illustration. "There are two styles. One style is very graphic-based, utilising the computer. The second style is based in photography utilising, in some cases, mandalas and symbols." The computer is her favourite tool. "It's as easy as drawing with a pencil. It's easier to play with." As a graphic designer, the sources of inspiration have been many. Paul Rand, manga and anime have formed an extensive library, along with ideas and inspirations picked up over many years in the bookshops of Paris. "I am 50 percent graphic designer and 50 percent illustrator." She likes being my own client, but not all the time. I begin within a style of upon me." With graphic design I like playing around within the constraints imposed imagery and notice afterwards that they follow various themes." These themes are never intentional. "The characters I create have identities projected onto them by the audience for my work. The little black character does not express anything. He is not human, but he might be a spirit or some kind of extra-terrestrial. I don't really care. It is not important." People relate to her work and regard it as cheerful and happy. "I want to take these notions and make them more bizarre. The characters are cute but they die, or misbehave, are lonely, and this allows me to mix feelings."

Combining design with the process of image-making gives Big Active art director Mat Maitland a wide range of creative possibilities. "I have always been excited about the image-making process, being surrounded by it every day. It's a natural extension of my design work and allows me to work across various media." Mat's distinctive photomontage style has been utilised on many Big Active projects, including music campaigns for Goldfrapp and Pleasure. "I like the fact that my images embrace both illustrative and photographic elements. Also, collage is such an organic way of working. You always end up surprising yourself with the final image. The possibilities are endless and the thinking very lateral."

Many of his inspirations can be traced back to the creative indulgences of the post-punk era. "My influences are based in an exotic fantasyland of pop culture, stemming from my teenage years in the 1980s. That time felt so futuristic and imaginative to me, particularly the movies and pop stars. I was obsessed with Prince and Michael Jackson, both of whom projected such an enigmatic other-worldly presence. Also, as a young teenager, you are experiencing things for the first time, in a dreamy, often naïve way, and the 80s offered me source material in abundance. I don't think any decade since has come close." Mat approaches his subject matter with a voyeuristic eye. "I tend to start off collecting material without thinking too much about the final image. I look at basic themes and objects and set about taking source photographs. These images along with my huge library of permanent material come together to form a final piece which sometimes takes weeks, sometimes minutes."

Mat
Maitland

Daniel
Stier

"I have always been a photographer," says Daniel Stier. "My work has never really changed since I was at college. I try not to be distracted by the work of other photographers, preferring to concentrate on what I want to achieve." His first approach has always been to document. "When I find a subject that interests me I take my camera and shoot it. I have been educated in telling stories photographically. I love working on the larger story that this affords."

Photography takes him to all manner of places he would not otherwise go. "The camera allows me to be more curious than I naturally am. It allows me to give greater depth to the subject. I am also looking at the atmosphere of any given place. I try to ask questions from an observational point of view." There is so much you can read into the work, so interpretations can differ. The process is simple, with no reliance on post-production, but a good deal of advance planning before the images are taken. "The camera is secondary to my being able to look at things I would not normally see."

Kristian Russell uses illustration to express the extrovert side of his inner self. Executing images that could be viewed as 'high glam', Kristian is looking to capture the essence of musicians such as Iggy Pop, who could be seen as living their lives to the full with an outwardly extravagant image. "I like the visual energy and, when I'm sitting drawing, I am looking for this attitude. It could be a disco energy but rock and roll at the same time. I don't want it to be bland." This is mixed with a fascination with the human form, physique and movement. After the physical comes personality – as exemplified in his depictions of women. "Women turn me on. These women are people I would like to know. In the past I have based my work on people that I knew. Now it's more like living in the world of a rock video and imagining what these people would be like."

The source for this work comes from a number of areas. Sometimes it is very specific, other times it comes from reflecting on the filter of the imagination. "Some of the work can be seen as pin-ups or fantasy." But the execution of a perfectly rendered human form is secondary to unravelling what is behind this mask. "In the past I would rush the work. Now it is more considered and I take more time. I guess this comes from searching for what's behind this pretence." The work attracts a variety of responses. "For some people it's the colour. For others it's the attitude. For me, I am trying to provoke a reaction in people. I want the audience to think that they would like to meet these people or be them. They're definitely aspirational." His own great wish is to see his work brought together in a single gallery space. "I have a desire to see my work appreciated in this setting. I am looking to push my work in this direction."

Kristian Russell

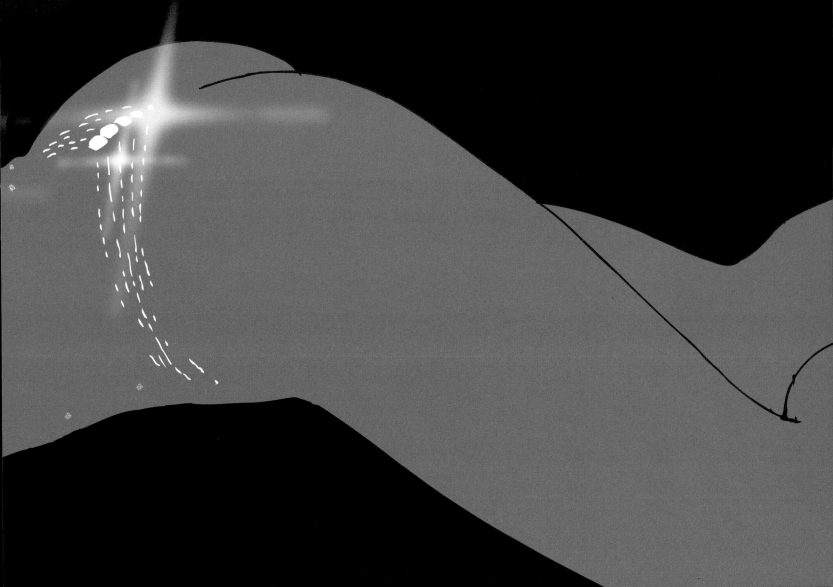

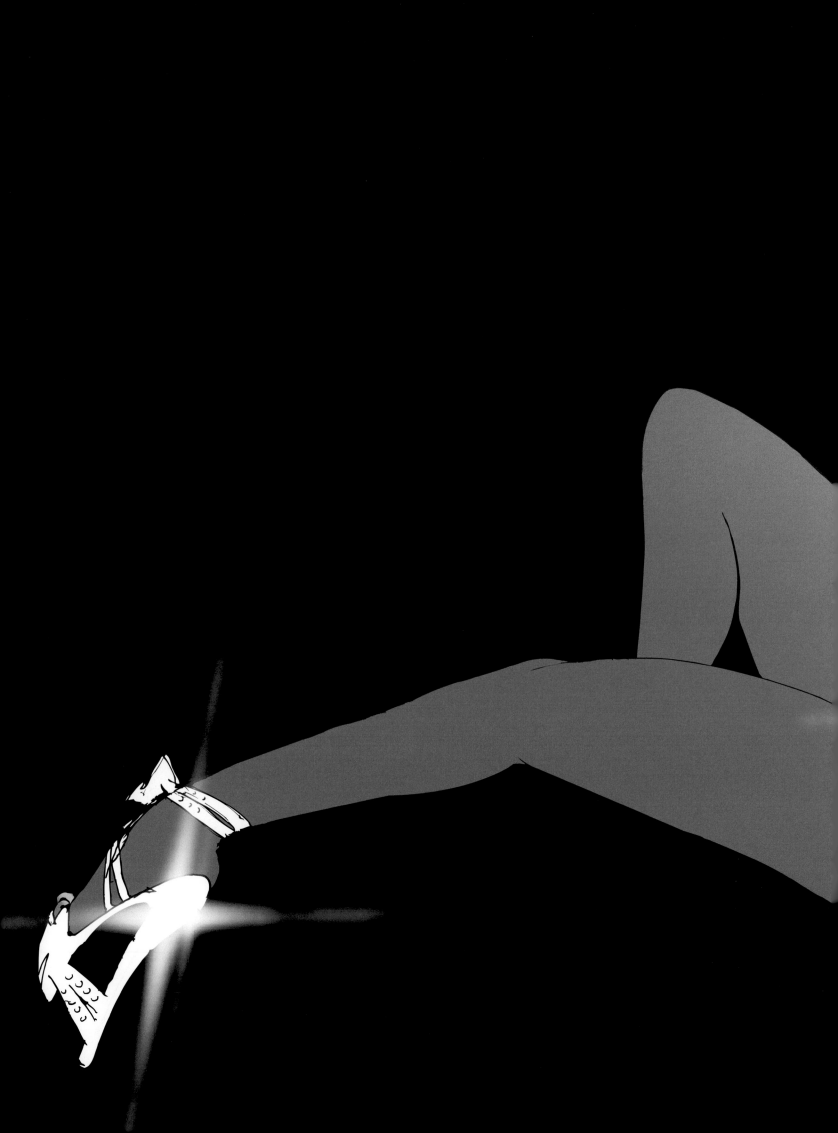

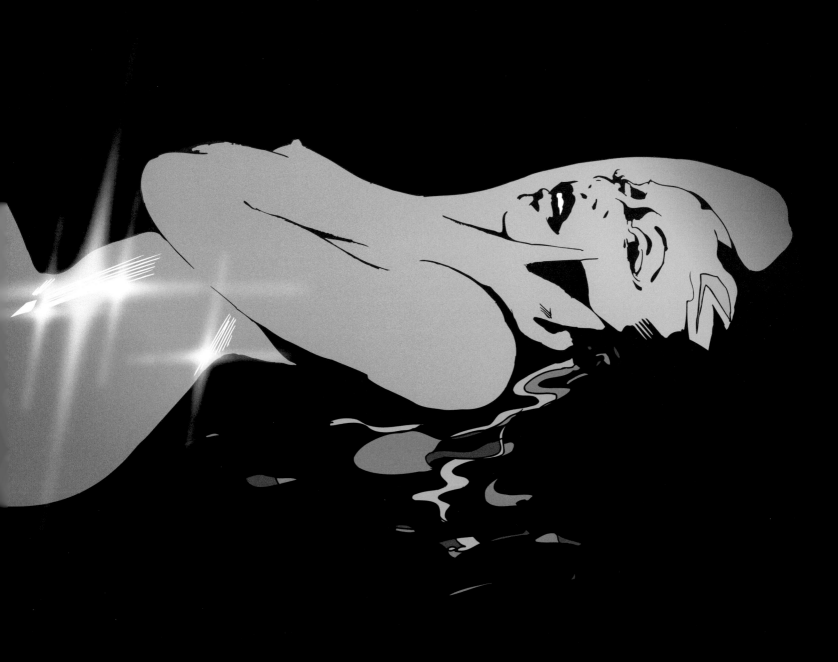

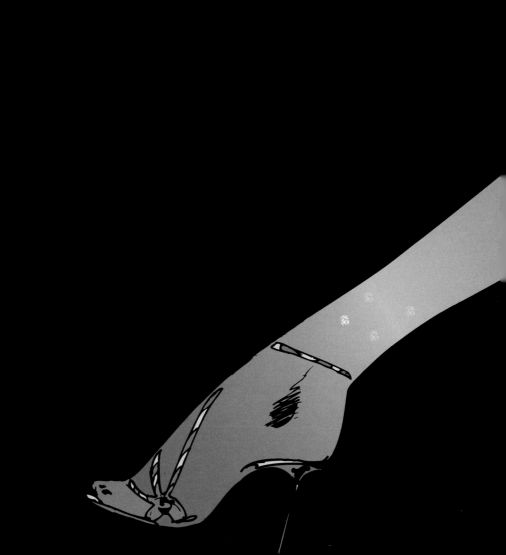

Will Sweeney regards himself as an illustrators' illustrator within the circle of his contemporaries. His main passion is drawing, and with quite a lot of detail. People he admires are from the past like Arthur Rackham, Aubrey Beardsley, and a host of luminaries from 60s and 70s illustration. "I like to think that I can be influenced by lots of different things, but stylistically there is a distinctive pull to psychedelia and punk." These influences have been part of his work since he was a teenager. "They have never left me. Creatively I am constantly striving to get to where I wanted to be when I was of that age. My style has developed, but the energy and passion are the same – that's the most important thing for me. I quite like the idea of something being out of focus in the mind's eye and trying to attain it and never being that satisfied with it." His work is inspired by the objects, artefacts, books and music that surround him. "I don't have time to keep a sketchbook of ideas-in-waiting. However, something may come up when I am doing a project that doesn't fit and I make a written note of it." Will would love to paint more, though it's rarely commercially viable. Illustration offers an escape into fantasy – but not without its own dark pull. "I don't think I could not do it and this obsession has never left me. Reality and fantasy need to have a balance struck between them. The work needs the reality of ugliness to make the fantasy believable."

Will
Sweeney

Simon Henwood

Simon Henwood's practice as a conceptual artist, designer and illustrator has been motivated by the sign of innocence. His dogged exploration of childhood is represented in the arts establishment publishing world and his second film, *Alice*, explored how the sought to establish a dialogue with a non-adult audience, the responsible publication of children's books sought to delve into the pleasing conceptual enthusiast of the artist. His career, 'exploring the child's unbridled enthusiasm, whilst drawing out the wonders and capabilities of young minds. Simon conjures the anxieties, pressures and expectations of youth and childhood.

He has continued to adopt the child's single-minded enthusiasm by keeping in touch with the child's unbridled enthusiasm as take up the sign of innocence, and different media. Through the child's exhibitions and museum shows in the U.K., U.S, Europe and Japan, his films have featured in solo shows such as Sonic Youth, 1997 pop and Tindersticks, a quarterly music video, the Purr publishing company, the Purr publishing project also spawned an exhibition programme and art releases for artists such as Sonic connection, he produced music; video; launched pur magazine, a quarterly label for record and film, animation that has taken thirteen before and childhood.

He is a writer and illustrator in London, New York, embarking on in London, this media mixed in publishing and the fields of publishing before he worked as he mixed dedicated to books of Beijing this through illustration, before publishing and 1963 he Tindersticks. Through limited-edition rough labelled first media.

"My work is developed through a wide area of disciplines and activities and often centres on the subject of childhood and adolescence," says Simon Henwood, "I studied mixed media, painting on film, painting and as a continuation of the artist's career," — a discipline of childhood and childhood.

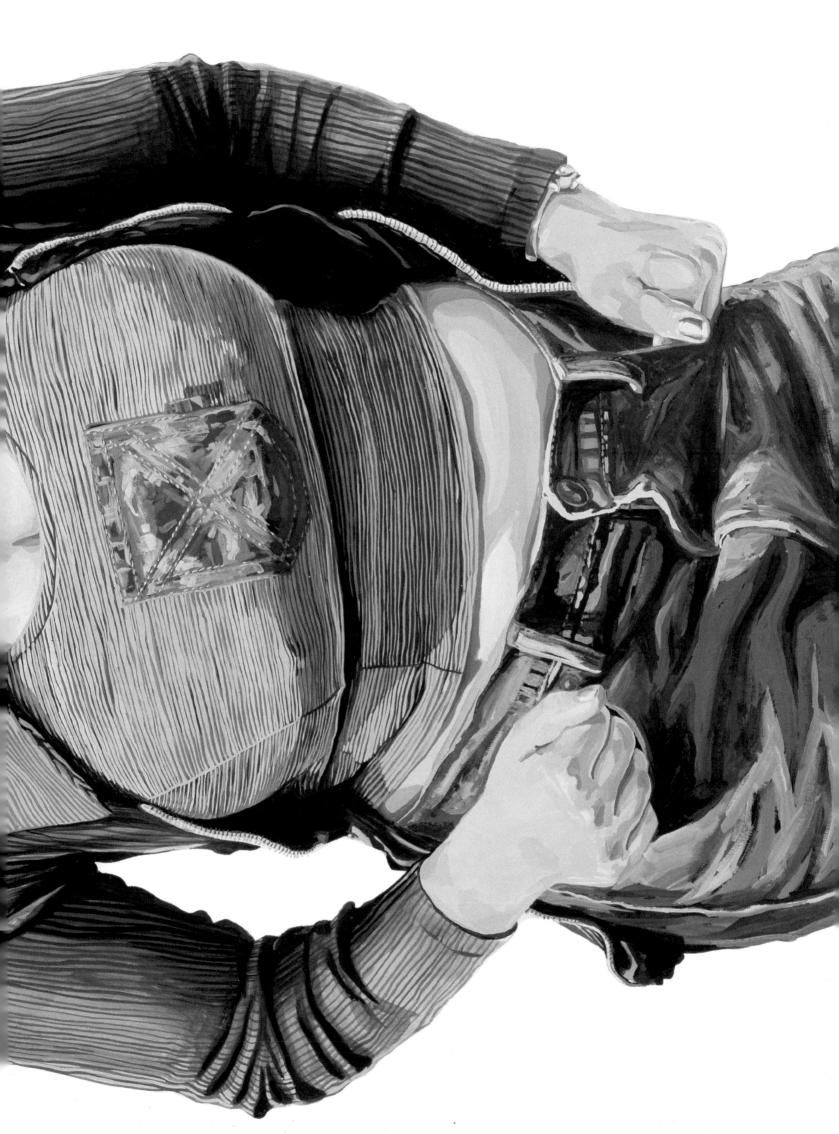

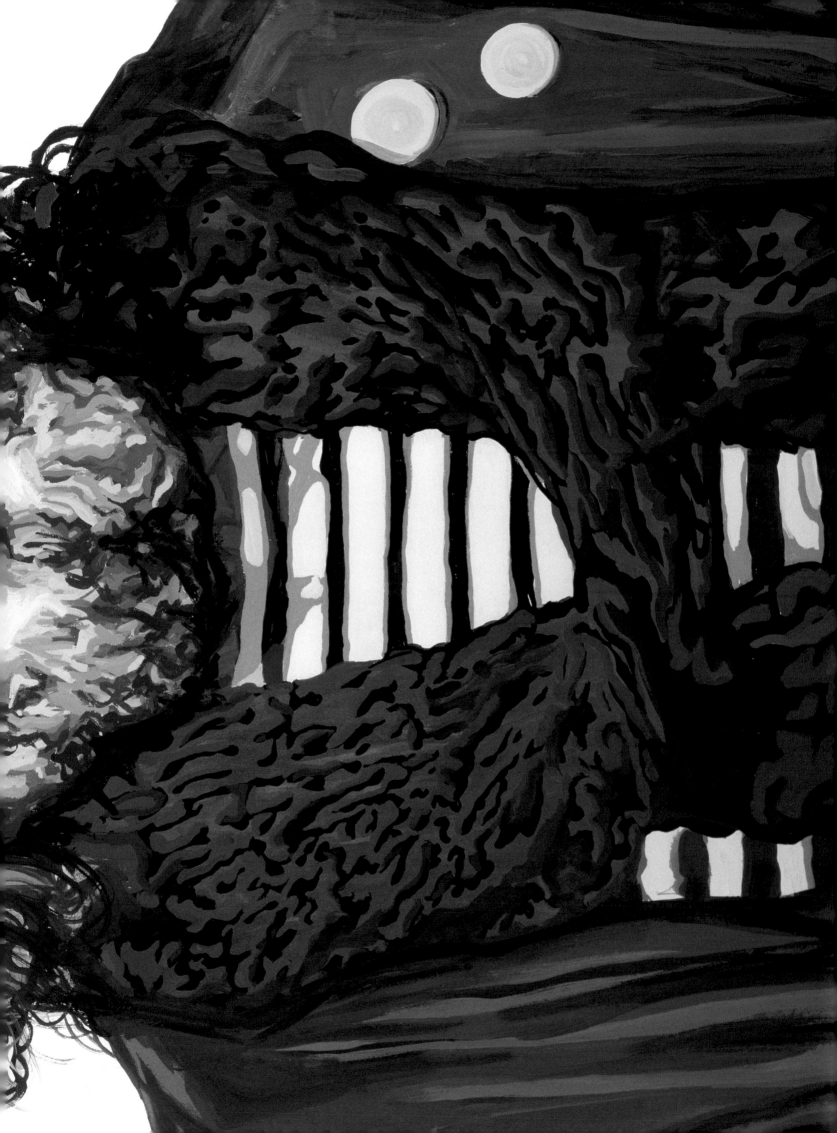

Rachel Thomas creates in a number of media, giving her ample opportunity for overlap and exploration. "I work in so many materials that require different approaches that sometimes one project will feed the ideas of another." Set design might inspire something she can take further in photography. "I like the confidence of being able to do something really minimal and in repetition. It's not fine art but it serves to respond to a commercial brief, something that I enjoy receiving. I'm so into having a brief to work with. I'm now working in film, on a book project, along with shooting fashion. They all cross over through me but all demand different things."

What always creeps in through all this activity is some kind of magic, fairy tale, fantasy or escapism, along with a pervading presence that nods towards Cecil Beaton and Jean Cocteau, two sources of admiration and influence. She does not wish to make things that reference reality, but favours artifice and experiment. "A lot of the work I do comes out of accident, lack of knowledge and my own technical limitations." Her work is full of idiosyncrasies and leaps into the unknown. "I studied fine art but I made photographs and film for my degree. I wanted to be an artist but didn't know how to be an artist in the real world. I fell into designing fabric prints, ending up making a film for the same fashion label. This in turn led to directing pop promos, but simultaneously I was making a living in window display." She enjoys being swept along into different areas. "Some people have a real problem with me not doing one thing. Others appreciate it. Doing commercial work allows me to hide my emotions away. Emotions are not a function of my work."

For Rachel, true art lies between the idea and the process, and in taking risks without fear of being out of one's depth. "At college I was taught that it was not about the form it was about the concept. Whatever form suits the idea then use that form. Don't get stuck in one medium. On top of this, working commercially has been so liberating. I just work."

Rachel Thomas

PHOTOGRAPHY BY DAN TOBIN SMITH

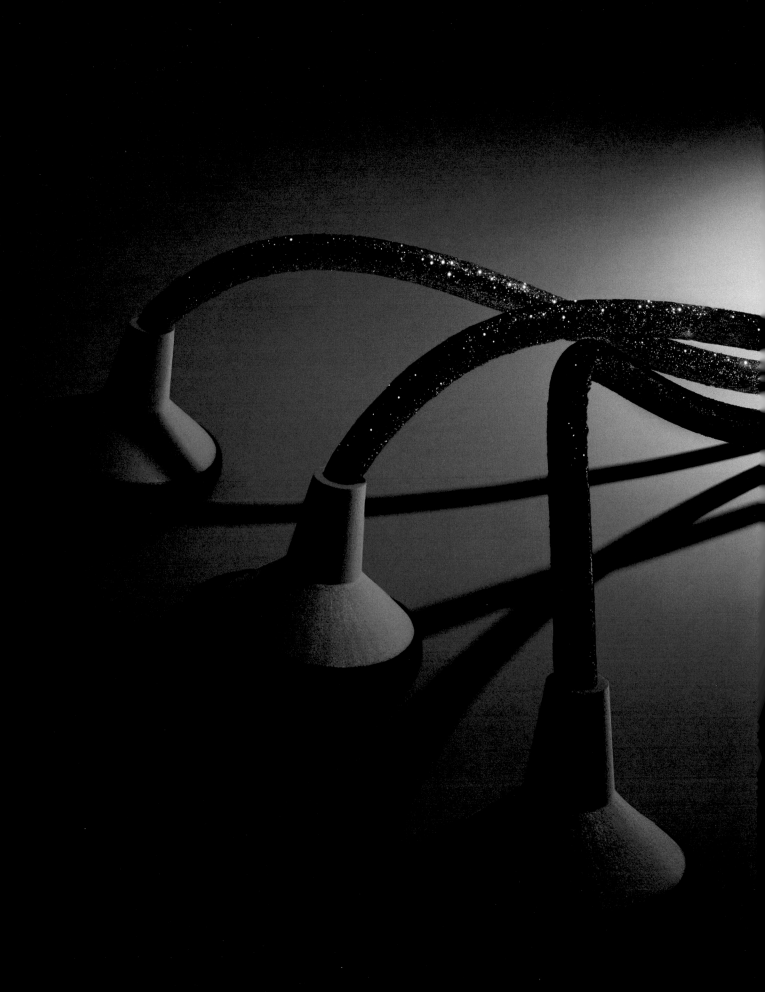

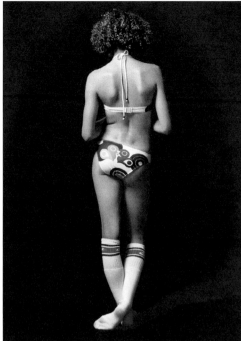

JG4B, 2004–05
Where art meets flesh:
promotional imagery
from Jasper Goodall's
ongoing collaboration
with swimwear designer
Louise Middleton.

THE COMMERCIAL WORLD of photography and illustration is consistently driven by hunger for originality and passion for change. As in any market, commerce appropriates the new in order to invigorate, whether launching new products, or refreshing established brands. But if brands consume originality by definition – nothing can remain fresh beyond its natural span – the upside of the style vacuum created by this endless consumption of the new is that it encourages diversity of demand, creating a thriving landscape for the commercial artist that embraces all manner of styles and techniques. An image-hungry market naturally benefits commissioners and commercial artists alike, so long as their own output is constantly topped up with new and distinctive styles of work. Many careers have been built in this way, where the alert artist has recognised the need to constantly reinvent and explore new avenues.

"We firmly believe artists should be encouraged to take control of the authorship of their creativity, exploiting opportunities to broaden the market for their work." There are many fine examples of such diversification, both within and outside the Big Active stable. The characters who inhabit Pete Fowler's World of Monsterism and James Jarvis's World of Pain broke free of the traditional constraints of commercial illustration to become wildly successful, pioneering model figures. Such artists hold the enviable position of being totally self-sufficient whilst free to pursue the commercial projects that most interest them. Many outlets have sprung up to embrace this new market. In Paris, the eclectic Colette design boutique brings together clothing, accessories, cosmetics, music, literature, food and drink alongside permanent exhibition space. Similar retailers vie for the attention of aesthetically-minded consumers from London to New York to Tokyo.

In the last decade, the internet has been a huge factor in promoting the work of commercial artists to unprecedentedly large audiences, and in establishing a vibrant dialogue between Western commercial artists and their peers and 'fans' in the Far East – most notably in Japan and Hong Kong. Many artists' reputations have gained extra cachet for their acceptance in these new territories. Crucially, this commercial and creative cross-fertilisation has done nothing to diminish the desirability of their art. As the world grows smaller, we are witnessing a global cultural bring-and-buy, where emblems and motifs from previously alien societies are eagerly consumed and re-imagined for ever-wider audiences. Photography, graphic design and illustration have become so intertwined it is often impossible to see where one stops and the rest begin. Digital imaging is at once a great leveller and an unremitting creator of fresh demand.

**Helmut the Hot Dog Man
by Will Sweeney, 2005**
This mustard-keen action
figure is released by
Amos, accompanied by
the illustrated comic,
Tales from Greenfuzz,
also by Will.

World Cup footballs, 2002
Kate Gibb (top) and
David Foldvari (bottom)
FIFA-approved World Cup
2002 collectable footballs.
Concept and art direction
by Paintura/Stoique, Tokyo
for Puma.

Klong, 2005
Simon Henwood's
loveable plush toy,
released on the
Playbeast Label.
"A Klong cannot see or
hear you, but senses
your kindness."

Exciting creative opportunities are emerging as artists engage with an increasingly wide range of commercial contacts to explore new design solutions. Big Active has a solid commitment to this process, as winessed in the case of Jasper Goodall. There has always been a healthy demand for prints of Jasper's work, but a recent collaboration with swimwear designer Louise Middleton has taken his art into an exciting new environment. His JG4B range is now entering its second season. "This wearable art drips high value and luxury; words evoked on seeing Jasper's illustrations. In the future we plan to develop the idea further into a range of items associated with the beach and poolside living." An equally organic meeting of art and commerce is Simon Henwood's irresistible plush toy, Klong, a shapeless, selfless being whose welcoming arms are designed to hug, and whose internal organs are, quite literally, all heart.

"In both cases, it is a matter of understanding the needs of a unique product, researching the right producer and enabling it to go into action. A readiness to talk to industry can assist in the development of ideas from the wildest margins of the imagination and onto the shelves of stores around the world."

The willingness to go the extra mile, and seek new opportunities outside traditional commercial art channels is key to the Big Active philosophy. "People have the same subjective responses to the work whether it exists in an art gallery or as a piece of fabric design. There is a greater visual literacy then ever before, and this has been aided by a blurring of the lines between all forms of communication." It is gratifying that, at a time when instant pictures can be made in all kinds of conditions by anyone with the right mobile phone, there is a higher level of genuine appreciation for the skill of the working artist.

"We are very conscious that there is a wider market for the work of the artists we represent. This is apparent in the number of people who make contact wanting to know where they can consume the work beyond a record cover or editorial. This might have been the case for previous generations of image-makers, but we make a point of harnessing the benefits that this demand can bring." The creative landscape has changed in a positive way, the old boundaries between client and supplier have been blurred. "The client is now coming to the commercial artist not only to commission, but also as a customer for the products the artist has created. One could argue that this is a new form of communication, with the commercial artist now in charge of the terms of business." This spirit of collaborative playfulness, allied with sound business sense, forms the basis by which we seek to invigorate, invent – and seduce.

**Product of God
Packaging, 2004**
Freshly stickered artists'
prints await despatch.

Thanks &

We would like to thank all the artists who have produced work specially for this book and also those individuals whose generous enthusiasm, support and guidance has contributed to its production, especially Robert Klanten and everyone at Die Gestalten Verlag, Mark Reynolds, Daniel Mason at Something Else, Ann Harrision at Harrisons Entertainment Law, and David Hitchcock at dB#m. Deepest thanks are also due to all those whose efforts and organisation behind the scenes at Big Acitve have helped turn this project into reality:

Richard Newton, Greg Burne, Bianca Redgrave, and Markus Karlsson for his assistance. Thanks also to Rob Mills and everyone at FTP Creative for scanning, and Tony Gibson for photographic assistance. The title was inspired by a conversation with Jocelyn Bain Hogg.

We would also like to specially mention Mark Watkins and Paul Hetherington, and to salute all the designers who have assisted at the studio, and especially all the photographers and illustrators who have worked with us on past projects. We would also

like to acknowledge our clients, the many record companies, magazines and advertising agencies who have supported Big Active, in particular those whose commissions feature in the opening sections of this book: Mute Records, Alison Goldfrapp, Basement Jaxx, XL Recordings, Mark Barrott, Titanium Music, 679 Recordings, Universal/Island/Mercury, WEA/London, Parlophone, John Chuter and The Echo Label, Fred Ball, Sony BMG, Roma Martyniuk, Marc Baum, Dazed, Deborah Bee, Chris Sanderson and Martin Raymond at Viewpoint.

The following artists would like to thank those who have contributed to the production of their individual work contained in this book:

VAVA RIBEIRO (82-89): Styling by Ciro Midena & Lara Gerin, modelled by Bernardo, Paula Guillen & Camila Dubay
SHIV (90-97): Photography by Clare Shilland, modelled by Stella
ERWAN FROTIN (98-105): Retouching by Vincent Rochat. Thanks to Francis Ases, Philippe Dufour
PATRICK IBANEZ (122-129): Modelled by Greta Slezakova, make-up by Huê-Lan Van Duc

DANIEL STIER (148-155): Thanks to Jim Goldstein
RACHEL THOMAS (178-185): Photography by Dan Tobin Smith at The Katy Barker Agency. Retouching by Russell Kirby. Colour conversion by FTP (Digital). Photographic assistance by Michelle Grant
JASPER GOODALL (187): JG4B Look book, 2005 (detail). Photography by Josh Olins, styling by Clare Richardson, modelled by Angel @ Select

Respect is also due to the street artists we accosted on Shaftesbury Avenue one cold winter's night for our handsome pencil portraits (40-45).

Head, Heart & Hips features the work of:
GERARD SAINT
MAT MAITLAND
RICHARD ANDREWS
JASPER GOODALL
RENE HABERMACHER & JANNIS TSIPOULANIS
KATE GIBB
VAVA RIBEIRO
SHIV
ERWAN FROTIN
KAM TANG
DAVID FOLDVARI
PATRICK IBANEZ
GENEVIEVE GAUCKLER
DANIEL STIER
KRISTIAN RUSSELL
WILL SWEENEY
SIMON HENWOOD
RACHEL THOMAS

www.bigactive.com

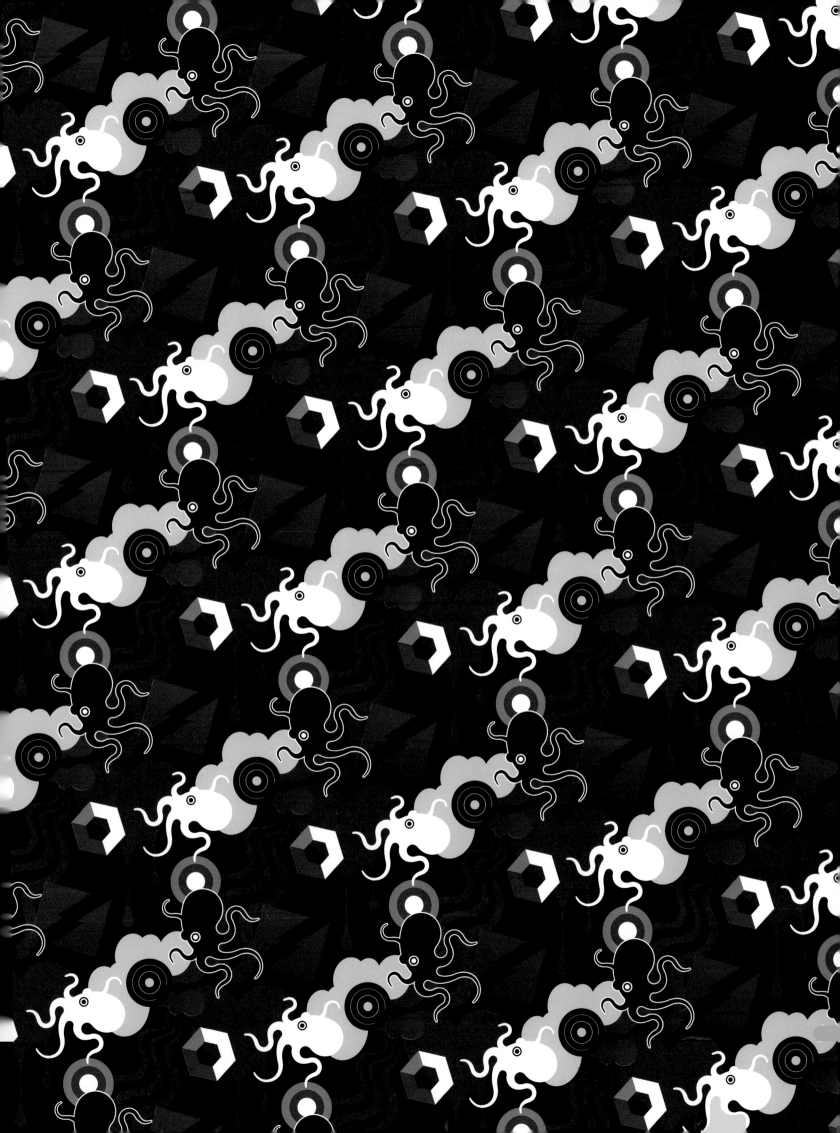

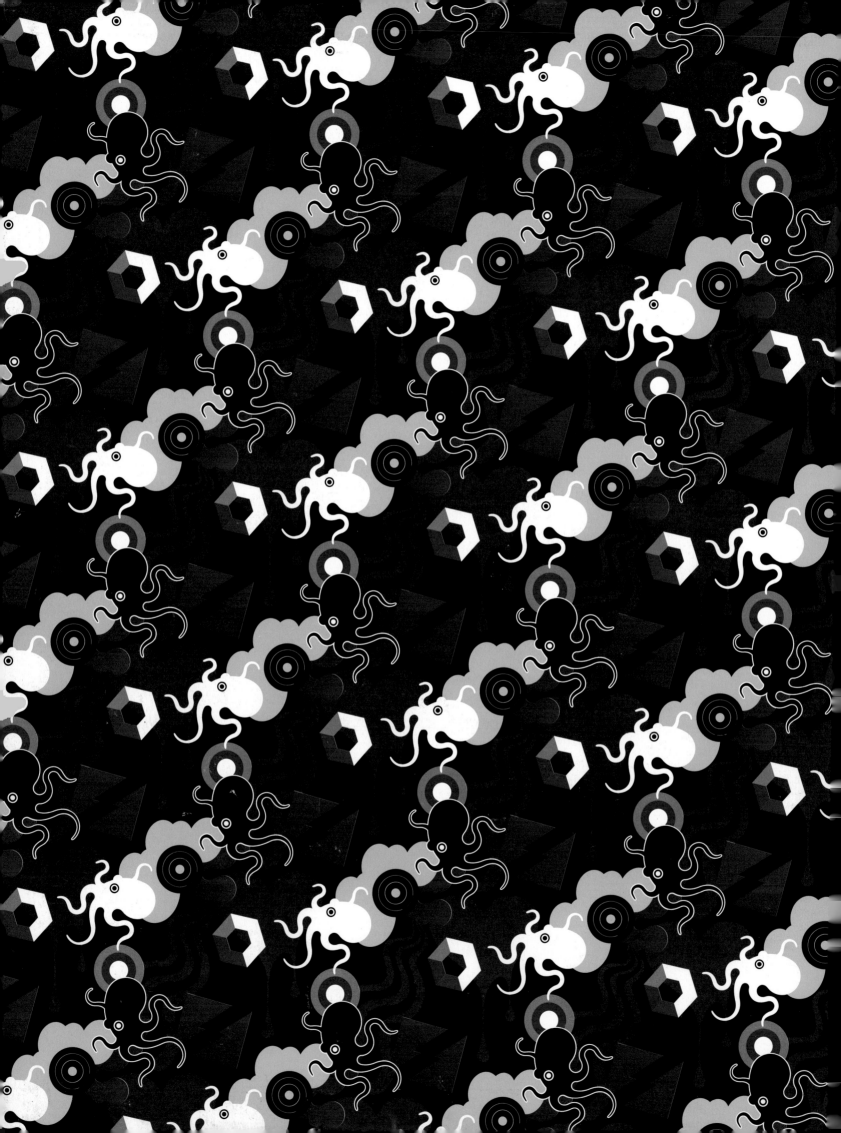